Poison Trees

etchings by Philippe Saltel
texts by Mathew D. Staunton

The Onslaught Press

Published in January 2014 by The Onslaught Press, 11 Ridley Road, OX4 2QJ

ISBN-13 978-0-9927238-2-8

Printed by LightningSource.

The first edition of **Poison Trees** emerged from Lilatelier and Paris Ateliers in October 2010. It was a portfolio of etchings printed on 250g Velin Reina paper by Philippe Saltel at his studio in Les Lilas, and accompanying texts by Mathew D. Staunton, typeset by Pierre Bérard on the Rue des Arquebusiers.
It was limited to 20 copies.

An exhibition of framed spreads from the portfolio took place at the Centre Culturel Irlandais in Paris in April 2011.

I was angry with my friend:
I told my wrath, my wrath did end.
I was angry with my foe:
I told it not, my wrath did grow.

from 'A Poison Tree' by William Blake

your wedding band
clicks up the stairs

a temple block
that fills the house with sound

a stream of piss
meanders out
between your feet

while you pretend
to study trees

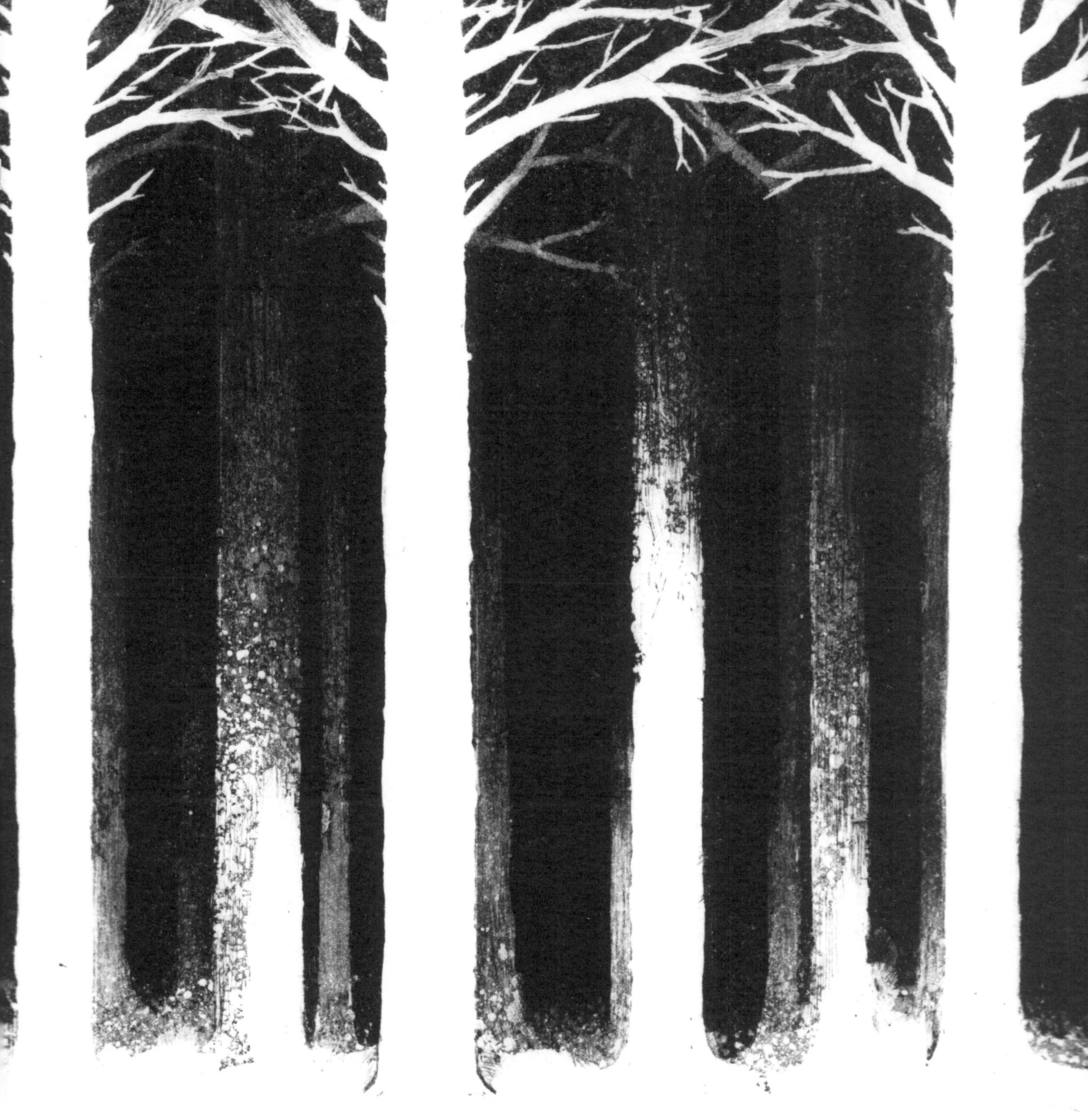

without a candle
to your name
but too afraid to leave the door unlocked
you plucked me
out of bed

with burning newspapers
to light the way
we processed down the garden
to the tree

and dug for all the keys
I'd buried in the morning

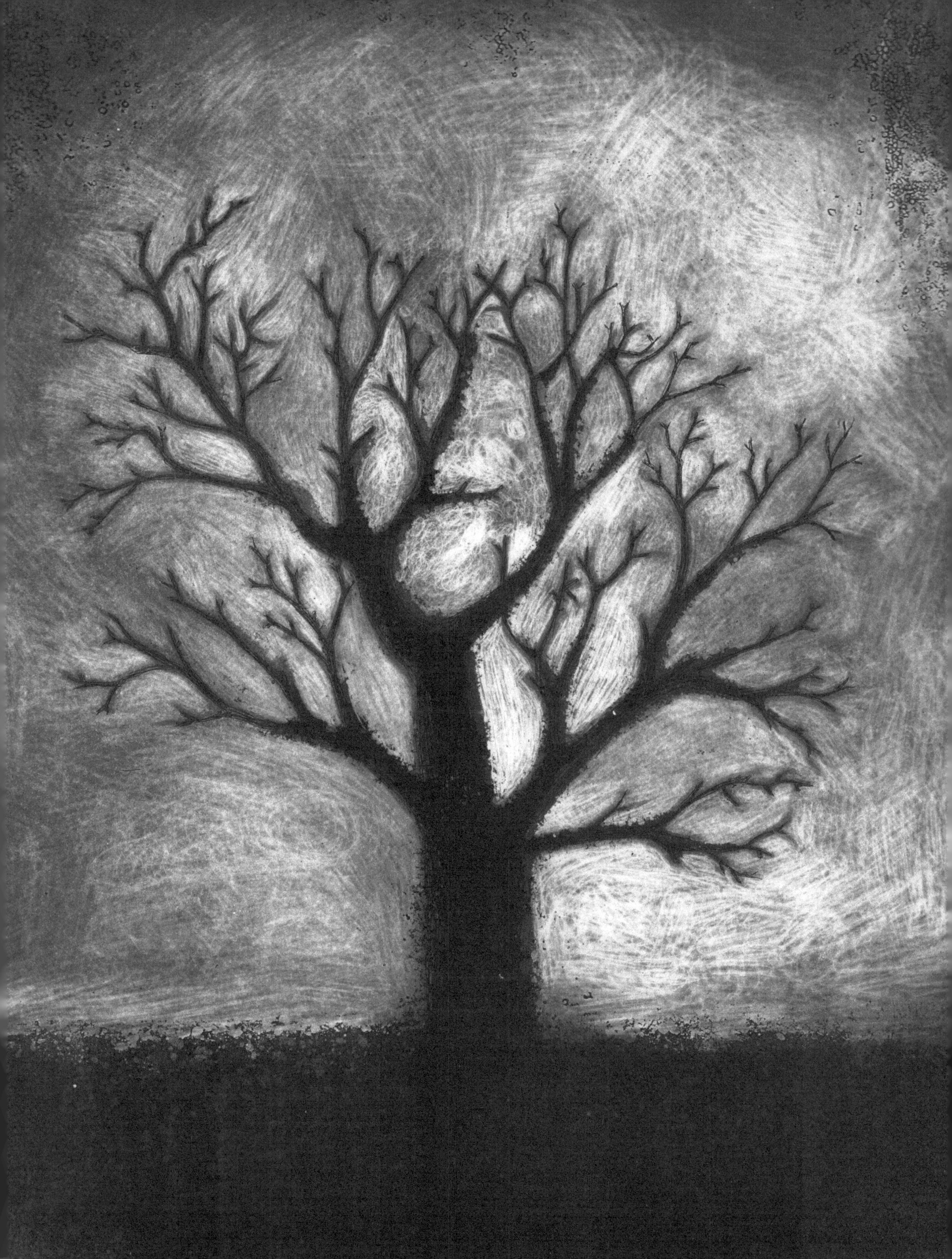

in the hyphenated
space between
the here and there

you made
a plastic tree

exploding shards of green and red

to punctuate
the year

stroking
every other day
you found your faith in god knows what

and mapped the orchard

apportioning
each Chestnut Crab
and Bramley

parcelling your family
and farm

I got the Pixies
and a bit of broken wall

but lost a sister

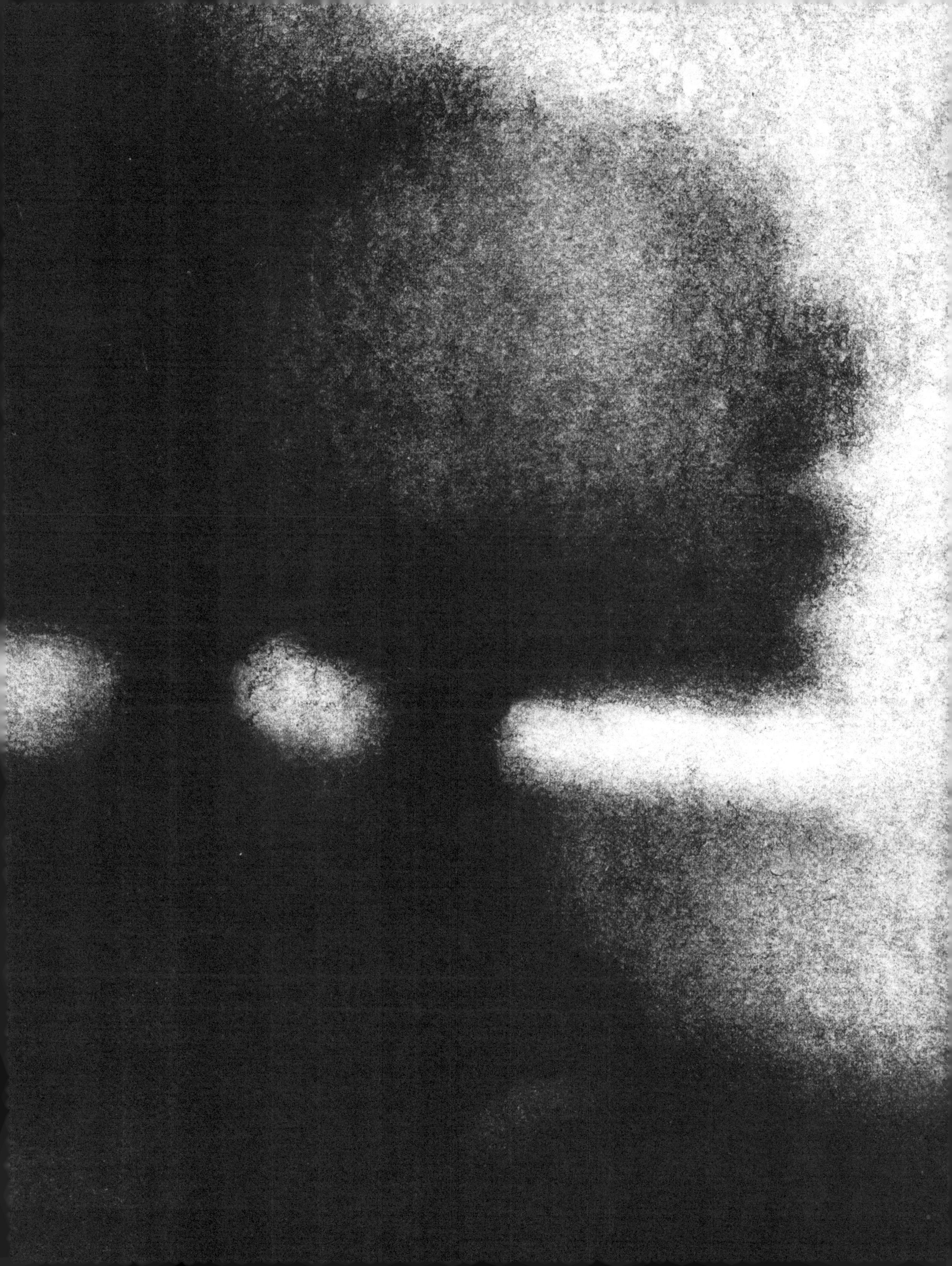

you scrumped
with men in shifts
and gleaming forklift trucks

to pile the table high with fruit

my tiny crimes
can’t hold a candle
in this light

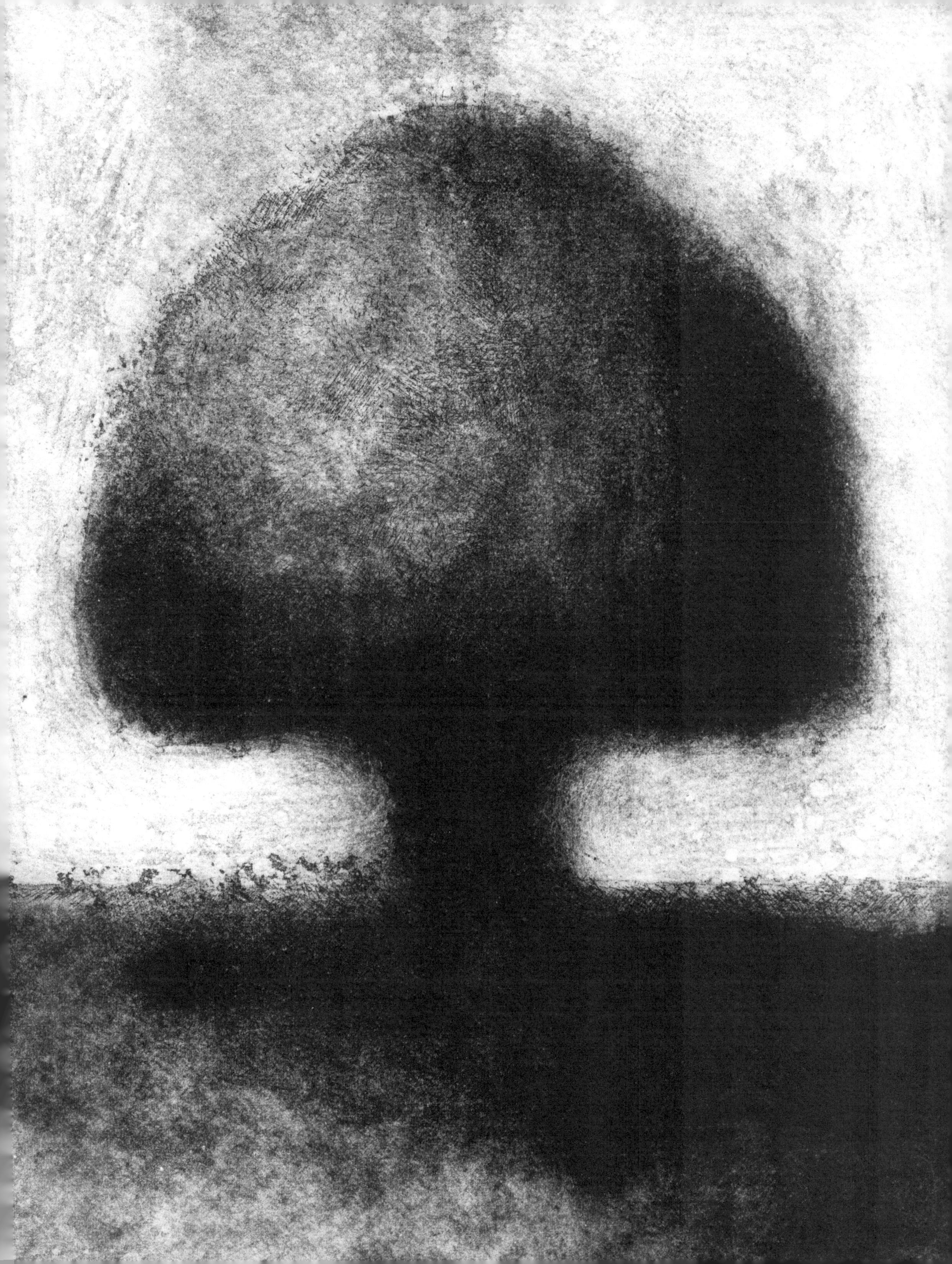

headlong
in a mucky field

patibulum of loss
across my back

I died an arm's length
from the tree

before my cheek
had touched the earth

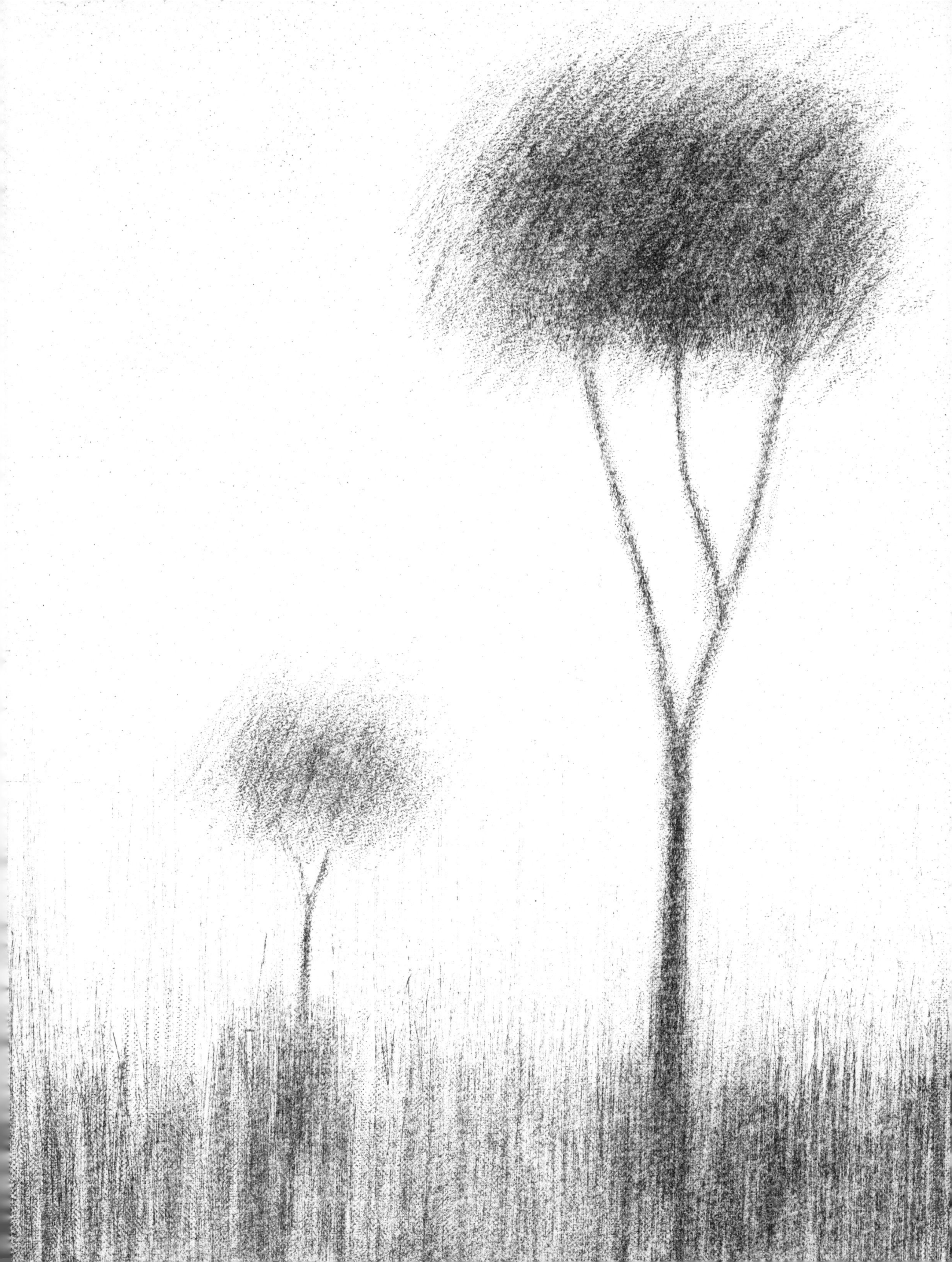

a sapling
in a Coolock park
where trees from Switzerland
are letterforms
my father used

an open bracket
interjecting
in an unknown font

a breath

and then I push off
into town
to look for closure

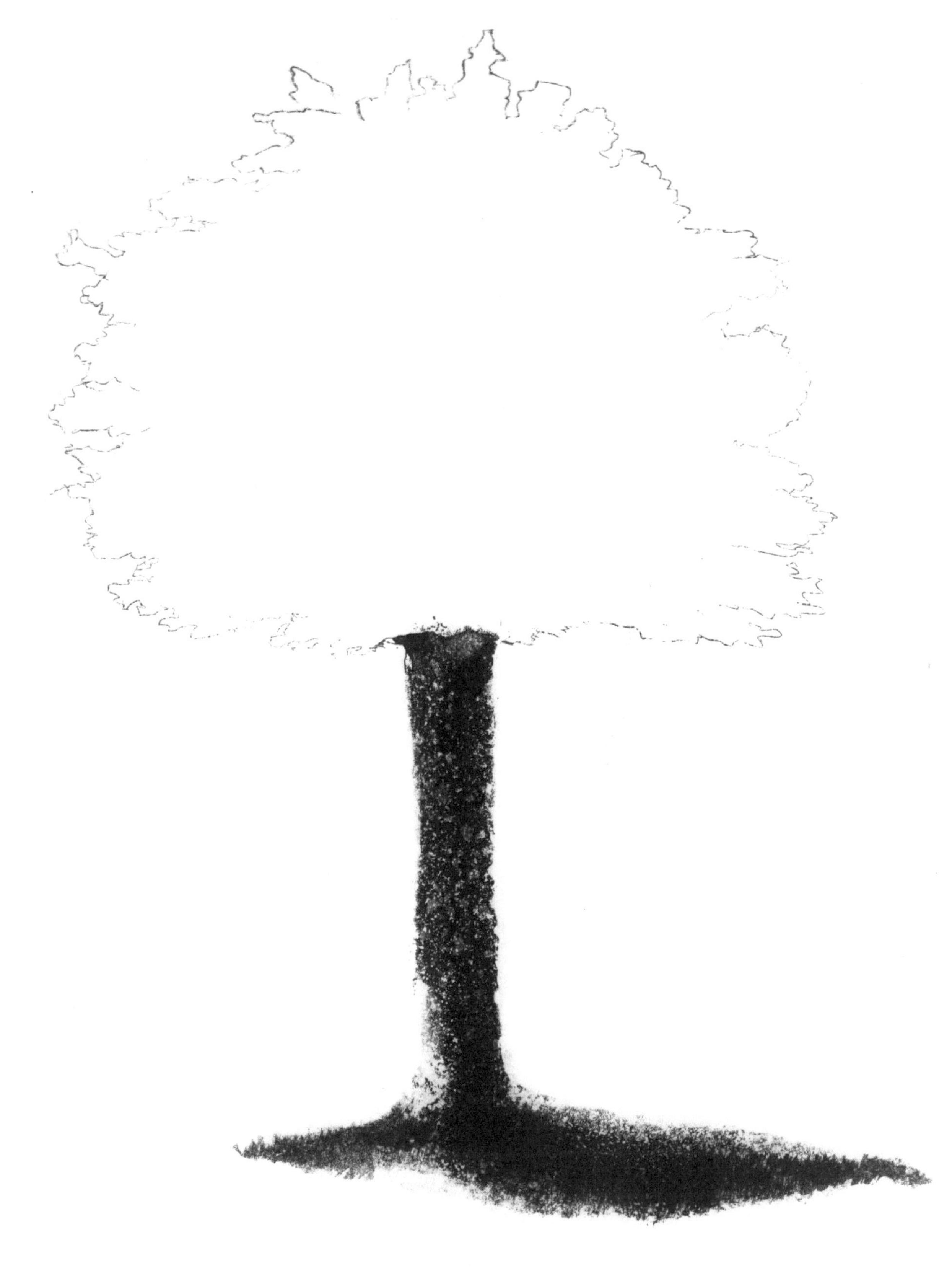

www.ingramcontent.com/pod-product-compliance
Lightning Source LLC
LaVergne TN
LVHW071630100826
845154LV00007BA/126
9780992723828